PRAGUE

KNOPF CITYMAP GUIDES

P9-CQU-310

CONTENTS

Welcome to Prague!

This opening fold-out contains a general map of Prague to help you visualize the 6 large districts discussed in this guide, and 4 pages of valuable information, handy tips and useful addresses.

Discover Prague through 6 districts and 6 maps

A Staré Město
B Josefov / Letná
C Hradčany
D Malá Strana
E Nové Město / Vyšehrad
F Vinohrady / Žižkov

For each district there is a double-page of addresses (restaurants – listed in ascending order of price – pubs, bars, music venues and stores) followed by a fold-out map for the relevant area with the essential places to see (indicated on the map by a star ★). These places are by no means all that Prague has to offer but to us they are unmissable. The grid-referencing system (**A** B2) makes it easy for you to pinpoint addresses quickly on the map.

Transport and hotels in Prague

The last fold-out consists of a transport map and 4 pages of practical information that include a selection of hotels.

Thematic index

Lists all the sites and addresses featured in this guide.

Welcome to Prague!

A Staré Město
B Josefov / Letná
C Hradčany

D Malá Strana
E Nové Město / Vyšehrad
F Vinohrady / Žižkov

BUBENEČ
(PRAHA 7)

KORUNOVAC

JUGOSLÁVSKÝCH
PARTIZÁNŮ

Vítězné
nám.

ČESKOSLOVENSKÉ
ARMÁDY

POD KAŠTANY

MILADY   HORÁK

EVROPSKÁ

LE
(PRA

TŘEŠOVIC
(PRAHA 6)

DEJVICE

LETEN
SAD

SVATOVÍTSKÁ

MILADY HORÁKOVÉ

BADENIHO

NÁBŘ. EDVARDA BE

JELENÍ

MARIÁNSKÉ HRADBY

CHOTKOVA

ČECHŮ
MOST

PATOČKOVA

HRADČANY
(PRAHA 1)

N

JOSE
(PRA

PRAŽSKÝ
HRAD

MÁNESŮV
MOST

MYSLBEKOVA

KEPLEROVA

ÚVOZ

Malostranské
nám.

MALÁ TRANA
(PRAHA 1)

B

17. LISTOPADU

S

KARLŮV
MOST

STA
MĚ
PRA

C

STRAHOV
(PRAHA 1)

KARMELITSKÁ

BŘEVNOV
(PRAHA 6)

PETŘÍNSKÉ
SADY

SMETANOVO
NÁBŘ.

STRAHOVSKÝ
STADION

VANIČKOVA

ÚJEZD

VÍTĚZNÁ

MOST
LEGIÍ

NÁROD

PA

STRAHOVSKÝ

PETŘÍN
(PRAHA 1)

ŠTEFÁNIKOVA

A

MASARYKOVO
NÁBŘ.

D

JIRÁSKŮV
MOST

RESSLOVA

TUNEL

KARTOUZSKÁ

NO
MĚ
PRA

PLZEŇSKÁ

DUŠKOVA

PLZEŇSKÁ

LIDICKÁ

RAŠÍNOVO
NÁBŘ.

VRCHLICKÉHO

RADLICKÁ

NÁDRAŽNÍ

SVORNOSTI

SVOBOD

VYŠE
RA

VLTAVA

SMÍCHOV
(PRAHA 5)

E

PODOLSK

RADLICKÁ

SMÍCHOV

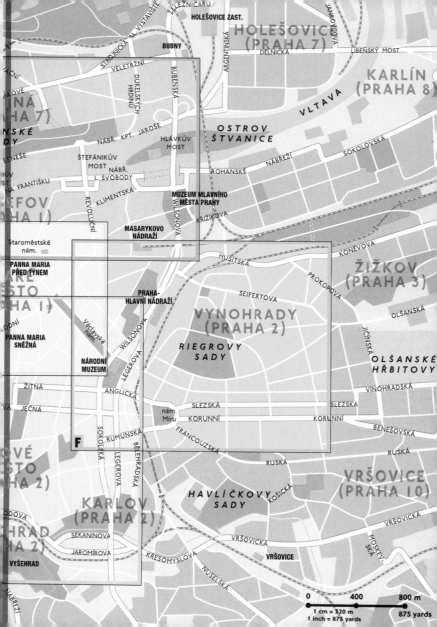

Winding alleys, galleries and passage-ways. The best way to escape the ceaseless throng of tourists is by getting lost in this maze of tiny streets. From Charles Bridge to Old Town Square, Staré Město, the historic heart of the city, is bursting with a panoply of styles: Roman cellars, dark Gothic towers, Renaissance houses, exuberant baroque façades. The weight of history is ever present. In Old Town Square the proud statue of Jan Hus revives the memory of the execution of ten Hussite leaders captured by the Catholics in the Battle of the White Mountain (1620).

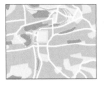

U DVOU KOČEK KONVIKT

RESTAURANTS

Klub architektů (A B2)
→ *Betlémské náměstí 5a*
Tel. 2440 1214
Daily 11.30am–midnight
Go down the steps in the courtyard opposite the Bethlehem Chapel, deep into the bowels of the earth, before reaching a series of vaulted cellars. The décor flirts with modernity but the thick stone 12th-century walls make it impossible to forget that Jan Hus once preached here. Czech specialties like *betlémská směs* (pork and vegetable stew) and international cuisine. Booking essential.
À la carte 100–150 Kč.
U Kamenného mostu (A B2)
→ *Smetanovo nábřeží 195 (entrance on Karlovy lazne gallery). Tel. 2409 7100*
Daily noon–1am
Two restaurants, two décors: one rustic for Czech cooking (duck and smoked chicken with red cabbage...), the other inspired by Provence, with a Mediterranean menu (chicken and ratatouille, fillet of sole...). In summer, a terrace at the foot of Charles Bridge.
À la carte 200-500 Kč.

Mlýnec (A B2)
→ *Novotného lávka 9*
Tel. 2108 2208
Daily 11am–3pm, 5–11pm
Italy, France, Bohemia but also India, Japan, Africa: Mlýnec offers a tour of the world's cuisines. Prague is the latest conquest for 'ethno-chic'. Sophisticated setting with a view of Charles Bridge. Dance floor.
À la carte 350–550 Kč.
U modré růže (A D2)
→ *Rytířská 16*
Tel. 2422 5873
Daily 11.30am–11.30pm
A huge 15th-century Gothic cellar, piano music and exquisite cooking (game, salmon) for a truly romantic evening. Good wine list. Around 700 Kč.

CZECH PUBS

U Dvou Koček (A D3)
→ *Uhelný trh 10*
Tel. 2422 1692
Daily 11am–11pm
Pilsner Urquell has flowed like water for centuries in the 'Two Cats'. The white walls display old posters advertising the brand and some vintage photos. On the tables are piles of glass mats: take one, put it down and a beer appears ... then another,

ÁRNA OBECNÍ DŮM

THEATER OF THE ESTATES

ST HAVEL'S MARKET

and so on, until saturation point. In the background, accordion tunes and the animated conversation of the locals. Good Czech cooking: *polévka* (soup) with cabbage, *guláš* (beef in sauce), *knedlíky* (pasta balls). À la carte 100 Kč.

Pivnice Radegast (A E1)
→ *Templová 2*
Tel. 232 82 37
Daily 10am–midnight
The thick cloud of smoke, the loud voices and laughter of the high-spirited customers set the tone more than the décor. Radegast (Moravian beer) on draft to wash down the generous helpings of food (one of the best *guláš* in town). A pub rapidly growing in popularity. 150–200 Kč/dish.

CAFÉS, PATISSERIES

Konvikt (A C3)
→ *Bartolomějská 11*
Tel. 2423 2427
Mon-Fri 9am–1am;
Sat-Sun noon–1am
Near Bethlehem Square. No trendy décor here, just some dark wooden tables and chairs for the lively young local customers, who laugh, smoke, drink (particularly beer) and

nibble on plates of breaded cheese or marinated herrings. For more peace and quiet, head for the room by the courtyard or the one in the cellar. Gambrinus, Pilsen, Kelt and Guiness on draft.

Kavárna Obecní dům (A F1)
→ *Náměstí Republiky 5*
Tel. 2200 6763 / 64
Daily 7.30am–11pm
One of the city's most spectacular cafés. Period candelabras, big mirrors, swathes of marble and metal, waiters in costume: the enormous hall has retained its 19th-century glory. Elegant ladies, businessmen and passing tourists mingle for a breather over a coffee (*káva* or *kafe*) or a pastry. Coffee 37 Kč. Internet corner.

Café café (A D2)
→ *Rytířská 10*
Tel. 2421 0597
Mon-Fri 10.30am–11pm;
Sat-Sun 11am–11pm
The brightest of all Prague's cafés, with big bay windows overlooking the street. A variety of drinks, snacks and pastries.

Café Milena (A D1)
→ *Staroměstské náměstí 22*
Tel. 2163 2602

Daily 10am–8pm
On the first floor, three small, subdued rooms for sipping tea or savoring a pastry while watching the world go by in Old Town Square. Coffee 40 Kč.

Odkolek (A D2)
→ *Rytířská 12 (No tel.)*
Mon-Fri 7am–8pm; Sat 8am–8pm; Sun 10am–8pm
Different types of bread, *sacher torte* (chocolate cake), *jablkový závin* (strudel) and *koláče* (fruit and poppy seed tarts) in one of the best patisseries in town. Cake 25 Kč.

NIGHTCLUBS, THEATER

Double trouble (A D2)
→ *Melantrichova 17*
Tel. 2163 2414
Daily 4.30pm–4am
A nightclub very popular with expatriates. In a maze of vaulted rooms, two bars, video screens and rock-pop music at maximum volume.

Karlovy lázně (A B2)
→ *Novotného lávka 5*
Tel. 2222 0502
Daily 9pm–5am
The former public baths turned into a gigantic nightclub, with three bars, three dance floors

(house, hardcore, hip-hop and 1960s sounds) and a post-industrial atmosphere (exposed pipes, old boilers). Live concerts 50–100 Kč.

Theater of the Estates (Stavoské divadlo) **(A** E2)
→ *Ovocný trh 1*
Tel. 2421 4339
Prague's oldest theater, built by Count Nostic in 1781. It was here, in 1787, that Mozart's *Don Giovanni* was first performed. Two centuries later Miloš Forman filmed *Amadeus* on the same spot. The theater was completely restored in 1992. Today it houses ballets, classical concerts and opera in rotation.

SHOPPING

St Havel's Market (A D2)
→ *Havelská*
Daily 8am–6pm
Havelské Město has been the domain of traders since the 13th century, and its market is still one of the prettiest in Prague. Colorful fruit, flower and vegetable stalls, but also Czech and Moravian crafts: dolls in traditional dress, wooden toys, embroidered fabrics and table linen.

The only relics of the eventful history of what was one of Europe's most important Jewish communities: six synagogues, the cemetery and the Jewish Town Hall, now retrieved by the tourist industry. Nothing remains of the labyrinthine old ghetto: in the 19th century the maze of courtyards and teeming alleyways gave way to wide and graceful avenues. The Renaissance, baroque and Art Nouveau styles rub shoulders on the façades of the upmarket stores in Pařížská. On the opposite bank is Letná Park, a perfect setting for a stroll, and, further north, Holešovice, a lively neighborhood with its roots in the industrial era.

HANAVSKÝ PAVILÓN

BAROCK

RESTAURANTS

Chez Marcel (B C3)
→ Haštalská 12
Tel. 231 56 76
Daily 8am–1am
A small corner of France in the heart of Prague. Foreigners from various countries meet here over a drink or a meal, under the benevolent gaze of a poster of football player Zinedine Zidane. On the menu: quiches, omelets, chicken, fried mussels. Wine bar in the basement. À la carte 200 Kč.

Red, Hot & Blues (B C4)
→ Jakubská 12
Tel. 231 46 39
Daily 9am–11pm
Cajun and Tex-Mex cooking (quesadillas, fajitas, nachos) with a soundtrack of American jazz or blues: live bands every night. Happy hour from 4–6pm, brunch every weekend. Eat on the terrace on the inner courtyard in summer. Dishes 300 Kč.

Rybí trh (B C4)
→ Týn Ungelt 5
Tel. 2489 5447
Daily 11am–midnight
A chic restaurant in a medieval courtyard behind Our Lady of Týn. Expensive, but recommended for its very fresh fish and seafood. Oysters, shrimps, monkfish, salmon, eel, shark, steamed or grilled as customers can choose the way they want it cooked. Terrace on the courtyard in summer. Dishes 300 Kč.

Pravda (B B4)
→ Pařížská 17
Tel. 232 62 03
Sun-Wed noon–midnight; Thu-Sat 11.30am–2am
A highly sophisticated restaurant near the Old-New Synagogue, with an adventurous clientele in search of exoticism. Recipes from Peru, China, Italy, Spain. Dishes 400 Kč.

Hanavský pavilón (B A3)
→ Letenské sady 173
Tel. 3332 6641
Daily 11.30am–1am
A charming rococo hunting pavilion (1891), shrouded in the wood on top of Letná Hill. On fine days, a delightful terrace with a view of the city and the Vltava. Seafood specialties. Dishes 600 Kč.

WINE BAR, CZECH PUB

U Golema (B B4)
→ Maiselova 8
Tel. 232 8165
Mon-Fri 11am–10pm; Sat noon–11pm

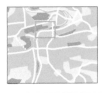

MARQUIS DE SADE

ROXY

BOTANICUS

A quiet, restful wine bar, popular with Prague's Jewish community. The strange names of some of the dishes – the 'Rage of the Golem', the 'Rabbi's bag' – refer to the old ghetto legend of the mythical Golem figure. Meat, fish and poultry dishes. À la carte 200 Kč.

Švejk (B B4)
→ Široká 20.
Tel. 2481 3964
Daily 11am–11pm
One of the many places in the city paying tribute to the Good Soldier Švejk, hero of the popular novel by Jaroslav Hasek. Wood trim, old posters, vintage prints for a pleasant tavern with good Czech cooking: *bramboračka* (potato soup), *buřty cibuli* (salami and onion), *pečené koleno* (shin of pork). À la carte 150 Kč.

CAFÉS

Barock (B B4)
→ Pařížská 24
Tel. 232 92 21
Daily 8.30am–1am
(Brunch: Mon-Fri 8.30–11.30am; Sat-Sun 10am–4pm)
Photos of models on the walls, designer furniture and a hip crowd of both locals and tourists. Good

selection of cigars (from cigarillos to vintage Davidoff at 350 Kč). Brunch, homemade croissants.

Dolce vita (B B4)
→ Široká 15. Tel. 232 9192
Daily 8am–midnight
One of Prague's few Italian cafés, for a real Italian espresso or a creamy cappuccino. Short food menu: panini, ham and melon, mozzarella salad...

BARS, NIGHTCLUBS

Kozička (B B4)
→ Kozí 1. Tel. 248 18 30
Mon-Fri noon–4am;
Sat-Sun 6pm–4am
Relaxed in the afternoon, lively and youthful at night. Krušovice (beer from central Bohemia) on draft, Slivovice (plum brandy). Short food menu (chicken, chili, salads). Dish 100 Kč.

Marquis de Sade (B C4)
→ Templová 8
Tel. 2481 7505
Daily 11am–2am
A huge red room decorated with odds and ends and round tables, frequented by young locals and expatriates eager for a good night out. Good atmosphere,

copious tobacco smoking, strong liquor, Czech beer on draft (Velvet, Kelt, Krušovice) and, sometimes, live music. Beer 25 Kč.

La Provence/ Banana Café (B C4)
→ Štupartská 9
Tel. 9005 4510/512
Daily 11am–1am
This is one of the city's most fashionable spots: a café-bar-restaurant, popular with American expatriates and Czech yuppies. Gogo dancers and heady techno rhythms. Piano bar (Tue), drag show (Wed), Jazz (Mon). French restaurant in the basement. Dishes 200–400 Kč.

Roxy (B B4)
→ Dlouhá 33
Tel. 248 26 390
Daily 7pm–4am
One of the last of Prague's mythical big nightclubs. Alternative look with cement walls, devoid of decoration, like an underground parking lot: techno, house, drum 'n' bass, jungle, trance, played by the best DJs in Europe. Strong liquor copiously consumed to remove any unwelcome inhibitions. Also film screenings, concerts, theater plays.

SHOPPING

Botanicus (B C4)
→ Týn Ungelt 3
Tel. 2489 5445 / 6
Daily 10am–7pm
The realm of plants and all things natural. Soaps, creams, perfumes, pots-pourris and a selection of craft goods from a village farm in Lysá nad Labem, to the northwest of Prague.

Kotva (B D4)
→ Náměstí Republiky 8
Tel. 2480 1111
Mon-Fri 9am–6pm;
Sun 10am–6pm
There is still a touch of Eastern Europe in the displays of this slightly old-fashioned department store, built in the 1970s. You will find, over five floors: toys, clothes, glassware, furniture, and food in the basement.

Pražký dům fotografie (B C3)
→ Haštalská 1
Tel. 2481 0779
Daily 11am–6pm
Gallery displaying more than ten exhibitions per year of work by Czech or foreign photographers (Kertesz, Weegee, Drtikol, Sander etc.). Exhibition catalogues, monographic studies, etc.

Perched on the side of a hill, the imposing Castle is actually a series of vast structures. Ever since its construction in the 9th century, the citadel has asserted itself as the seat of Bohemian power. It contains a Romanesque royal palace, Renaissance gardens, a Gothic cathedral, baroque churches, a convent... centuries of history and architecture. Outside the citadel, the Royal Way (Nerudova) hurtles down the slopes to the Vltava, leaving a string of wonderful baroque palaces in its wake. To the west of the citadel, the rococo splendors of Our Lady of Loreto border on Nový Svět, a timeless haven of rustic charm.

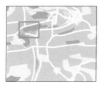

LVÍ DVŮR

U ZLATÉ HRUŠKY

RESTAURANTS

Sate (**C** A4)
→ *Pohořelec 152/3*
Tel. 2051 4552
Daily 11am–10pm
Customers sit at little square tables, in a big, vaulted white room decorated with colorful fabrics, to savor an authentic Indonesian meal (*nasi goreng*, chicken with coconut). Around 100 Kč.

Renthauz (**C** B4)
→ *Loretánská 13/179*
Tel. 205 11 532
Daily 11am–10pm (7pm summer)
Have lunch or dinner opposite the gardens of Petřín hill. On the menu, the classics of Czech cuisine: *vepřo*, *knedlíky*, *zelo* (pork, dumplings and cabbage). À la carte 155–185 Kč.

Lví dvůr (**C** C3)
→ *U prašného mostu 6/51*
Tel. 2437 2361
Daily 10am–2am
Soft lighting, exposed beams, sturdy wooden tables, bouquets of flowers: simplicity married to elegance. On the menu, *pražské selátko*: 'Prague pig' spit-roasted following a Renaissance recipe. 'Bohemia Sekt' wine,

produced especially for the restaurant. Around 300 Kč.

Peklo (**C** A4)
→ *Strahovské nádvoří 132/1*
Tel. 205 16 652
Daily 11am–4am
'Hell' – this was the monks' nickname for the cellar of the Strahov Monastery. Vaulted rooms, a host of alcoves, and good Italian-Czech cooking. Around 500 Kč.

U zlaté hrušky (**C** A3)
→ *Nový svět 3/77*
Tel. 205 15 356
Daily 11.30am–3pm, 6.30pm–midnight
The 'Golden Pear' offers sophisticated game specialties (duck breast with black pepper, haunch of venison with pears), in the cozy setting of a pretty 16th-century Gothic house in one of Prague's most elegant streets. In summer, meals are served under the centuries-old chestnut trees in the garden. Lunch menu 188 Kč. À la carte 800 Kč.

CZECH PUBS

Pivnice U Sv. Tomáše (**C** E3)
→ *Letenská 12. Tel. 536 776*
Daily 11.30am–midnight
In 1352, Augustinian

INEC STARÁ RADNICE

MALÝ BUDDHA

SHOP ON THE GOLDEN LANE

monks brewed the city's first beer here. These days, Braník (12°), an excellent dark beer, is on offer, as well as *guláš* cooked with beer. Live music at night. Around 200 Kč.

Hostinec Stará radnice (C B4)
→ *Loretánská 1*
Tel. 2051 1140
Daily 10am–10pm
A big slate attached to one of the large shutters in the entrance sets the tone: 'Old-style Bohemian cooking': garlic soup, *guláš*, *apfelstrüdel* and Pilsner Urquell on draft. Around 200 Kč.

U Černého vola (C A4)
→ *Loretánské náměstí 1*
Tel. 2051 3481
Daily 10am–10pm
A genuine *pivnice* in the heart of the tourist district. A long chest against the wall also acts as a bench. Don't hesitate to sit down beside the cheerful locals. Smoky atmosphere and Velkopopovický Kozel on draft, served to perfection. 30 Kč.

CAFÉS, TEAROOM

U Zavěšeného kafe (C B4)
→ *Radnické schody 7*
(No tel.)
Daily 11am–midnight
A tiny café-gallery resembling a cottage, halfway up the steps to the Castle. Sit at one of the solid wooden tables in the two small rooms, adorned with works by Jakub Kreji, to savor the robust *pivní sýr*, cheese with beer, served on a plate with butter, onions, sardines, mustards, paprika and pepper. Mix it all together and splash some beer on top before tasting. Coffee 25 Kč, tea 17 Kč.

Bistro Rudolf II (C D3)
→ *Zlatá ulička 30/31*
Tel. 2437 3658
Daily 10am–6pm (7.30pm summer)
Small bistro with a terrace. Pilsner Urquell on draft and Bohemian wines: whites (Muller Thurgau, Ryzlink vlašský) or reds (Svatovavřinecké, Frankovka). Glass 30 Kč, bottle 13 Kč.

Kajetánka (C C3)
→ *Hradčanské náměstí*
Tel. 57 53 37 35
Daily 10am–6pm (8pm summer)
On the way down from the Castle to the Nerudova. A spiral staircase leads to a small room with a terrace that offers a dizzying view of the red rooftops of Malá Strana. Tea, coffee, beer, wine, soft drinks and modest meals such as *kajetánka* steak (served with cheese and olives). Dishes 300 Kč. Wine 50 Kč (glass), 175 Kč (bottle).

Malý Buddha (C B4)
→ *Úvoz 45. Tel. 2051 3894*
Tue-Sun 1pm–10.30pm
As soon as the threshold is crossed, the tone is set: Zen-style music invites to a calm and meditative state – or not, but this is anyway a luminous and healthy spot, giving off good vibrations. Teas, energizing or relaxing, 35–80 Kč, vegetarian dishes 100-200 Kč. No smoking.

SHOPPING

Zlatá ulička (C D3)
The 'Golden lane' and its little colored houses seem to come straight out of a fairy tale. Legend has it that in the 18th century the street was home to 'goldmakers', alchemists searching for the secret of the philosopher's stone. Tourists turn up *en masse* to admire the work of the craftsmen who have set up shop here. Beware, prices are astronomical.

Salónek královny Žofie (C D3)
→ *Zlatá ulička Č. 18*
Tel. 2437 22 84
Daily 10am–4pm (6pm summer)
Clothes and accessories in natural products.

Česká lidová řemesla (C C3)
→ *Zlatá ulička 12 and 16*
Tel. 2222 0433
Daily 10am–7.30pm
Objects made of wood and wicker, eggs painted by hand, following a tradition dating as far back as the 6th century.

Galerie Nový svět (C A3)
→ *Nový svět 5*
Tel. 2051 4611
Daily 10am–6pm
A beautifully restored baroque house. Photographs of Josef Sudek, old glasses, drawings, prints and books on Czech artists (Josef Sudek, František Drtikol). Exhibitions of contemporary artists in the basement.

Antique music instruments / Icons gallery (C A4)
→ *Pohořelec 9*
Tel. 20 51 42 87
Daily 9am–6pm
Stacked high with old musical instruments and icons (with a certificate of authenticity and origin).

Nestled under Petřín hill, Malá Strana, the 'Little Quarter', slopes down from Hradčany to the Vltava in a cascade of red roofs interspersed with lush gardens and vineyards. In Malá Strana there has hardly been a new building since the 18th century, and the whole area, with its medieval layout of alleys, passageways, steps, and cul-de-sacs, is ideal for wandering. Its baroque palaces strive to outshine each other with statues and hidden gardens. A cable car ride leads to the top of the hill and the Belvedere, with a miniature replica of the Eiffel tower. In this romantic spot, time stands still as the Vltava casts its hypnotic spell …

CANTINA

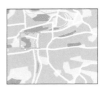

RESTAURANTS

Bohemia Bagel (**D** D3)
→ Újezd 16
Tel. 530 921
Mon–Fri 7am–midnight;
Sat–Sun 8am–midnight
Delicious bagels, toasted on request, plain or in various flavors (sesame, garlic or onion), filled with salmon and fromage blanc, chili… But also: soups, sandwiches, quiches, salads. Unlimited supply of coffee and soft drinks. Menu 69 Kč, coffee 35 Kč, Staropramen 20 Kč.

Cantina (**D** D3)
→ Újezd 38
Tel. 57 31 71 73
Daily noon–midnight
Homesick American expatriates have found their diner, and it has caught on with the locals too. Good Tex-Mex cooking (chili, burritos, fajitas). Cocktails (mojito, piña colada) 100 Kč. Dishes 100–200 Kč.

U sedmi Švábů (**D** C1)
→ Jánský vršek 14
Tel. 575 31 455
Daily
In winter, when the cold is merciless, the fireplace is a perfect refuge. Some wooden tables, a few benches and revitalizing

Czech recipes (goose liver with almonds, carp with garlic, roast beef with apples and myrtles). Around 150 Kč.

Nebozízek (**D** C3)
→ Petřínské sady 411
Tel. 537 905
Daily 11am–11pm
Its unbeatable location on the slopes of Petřín, hill attracts many tourists. International and Czech cuisine (roast pork, garlic soup). Reached via the Petřín cable car, get off at the Nebozízek stop. Dishes 200–400 Kč.

Bazaar Mediterranee (**D** C1)
→ Nerudova 40
Tel. 900 54 510/512
Restaurant: daily noon–midnight
Bar: daily 9pm–1am
Excellent restaurant with a Mediterranean touch (papillotte of salmon, stuffed eggplants). Lively atmosphere, drag show, parades of go-go girls… and boys. Dishes 200–400 Kč. In summer, eat in the garden or on the terrace overlooking the city.

Rybářský klub (**D** E2)
→ U sovových mlýnů 1
Tel. 575 33 170
Daily noon–10pm (11pm summer)

RVENÁ SEDMA | ZANZI BAR | OBSCHOD POD LAMPOUR

Freshwater fish specialties (trout, perch, carp). Spicy fish soup, carp with breadcrumbs (*smažený kapr*), or, at Christmas, with prune, grape and walnut sauce (*kapr na černo*). Riverside terrace. À la carte 200–300 Kč.

Čertovka (D E1)
→ U lužického semináře 24
Tel. 538 853
Daily 11.30am–midnight
Wonderful terrace by the Vltava. Full of tourists, but the view over Charles Bridge is stunning. Czech and international cooking. Around 300 Kč.

U modré kachničky (D D2)
→ Nebovidská 6
Tel. 537 905
Daily 11.30am–11pm
The 'Blue Duckling' has it all: sumptuous setting (vaults painted with frescoes, antique furniture, floral fabrics) and a menu paying tribute to the splendor of Bohemian cuisine. Delicious starters (roe deer paté), game specialties (duck, wild boar, venison), such as the outstanding *guláš*. Dishes 300–500 Kč. Another branch in Staré Město : Michalská 16.

CZECH PUB

Červená Sedma (D E2)
→ Na kampě 5
Tel. 539 985 / 533 483
Daily 11am–11pm
A genuine tavern. White and blue walls, dark wood tables, pretty carved benches, and a mixed clientele drinking wine or Staropramen on draft. A wide variety of Czech dishes, illustrated by photos, which will ruin the surprise for some, but are rather helpful if you are new to Czech cooking. Around 100–200 Kč.

CAFÉ

St Nicholas' Café (D D2)
→ Tržiště 10
Tel. 57 53 02 04
Mon-Fri 2pm–1am; Sat-Sun 4pm–1am
A quiet spot in the heart of the tourist district, ideal for meeting friends over a drink or coffee. Czech dishes (pork with croquette potatoes). Gin fizz 65 Kč, beer 30 Kč, dishes 170 Kč.

BARS, DISCOS

U malého Glena (D D2)
→ Karmelitská 23

Tel. 535 81 15
Daily 10am–2am (3am weekend)
Have a bite to eat on the ground floor (soups, sandwiches), before going down to the tiny, usually packed, vaulted, hall (come early if you want a seat). Cheerful crowd of enthusiastic thirty-somethings. Jazz (weekend), acid jazz (Thu), blues or Latin jazz (other days). Seven types of beer, Irish (Guinness, Murphy's) and Czech (Pilsner Urquell, Staropramen, Kelt, Velvet). Admission 70 Kč. Beer 35 Kč.

Malostranská Beseda (D D2)
→ Malostranské náměstí 21 (entrance under arcades). Tel. 53 90 24
Daily 8.30pm–2am
Concerts every night, by Czech or local groups (rock, jazz, country). Small CD shop (jazz and alternative rock). Admission 40–80 Kč.

Zanzi Bar (D D2)
→ Lázeňská 6
Tel. 0602 286 657
Daily 5pm–3am
The fashionable headquarters of young locals and American students who come to

be seen, but also to enjoy the endless list of drinks: 76 cocktails (including an explosive mixture based on absinthe). Small-scale concerts (jazz, rock, blues) several times a month.

SHOPPING

Pavel Truhlář Obschod Pod lampour (D E1)
→ U Lužického semináře 5/78 Tel. 02 727 691 89
Daily 10am–6pm
The clowns and goblins in the window sneer at passers-by with their creepy grimaces. The puppet tradition goes back to the 17th century and the Czechs are past masters of this art. It has given birth to vivid stock characters: the duo Špejbl and Hurvínenk (father and son), Kašparek (clown), the witch, Death, the Devil and other mysterious figures from a dark, enchanted world.

Galerie z (D E1)
→ U lužického semináře 7 and Letenská 1
Tel. 900 55188 / 544048
Daily 11am–6pm
The work of the greatest contemporary creators of Bohemian glassware.

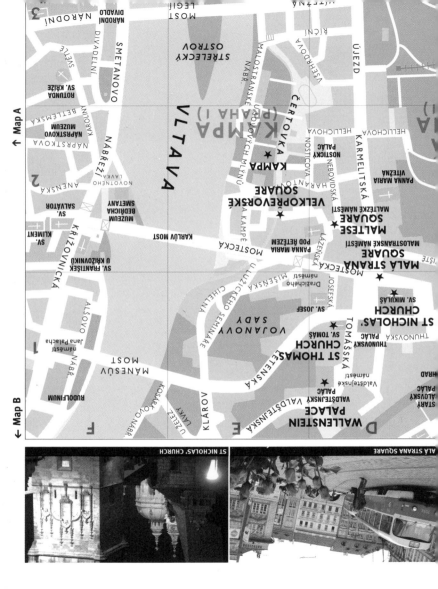

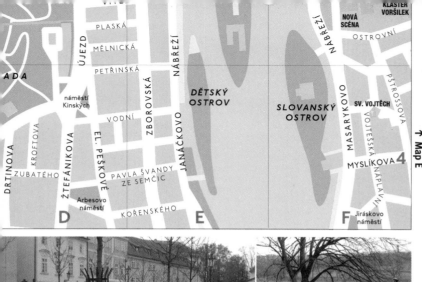

The map shows street names including PLASKÁ, MĚLNICKÁ, PETŘINSKÁ, NÁBŘEŽÍ, DĚTSKÝ OSTROV, SLOVANSKÝ OSTROV, SV. VOJTĚCH, NOVÁ SCÉNA, KLÁŠTER VORŠILEK, OSTROVNÍ, náměstí Kinských, VODNÍ, ZBOROVSKÁ, JANÁČKOVO, MASARYKOVO, MYSLÍKOVA, ÚJEZD, EL. PEŠKOVÉ, PAVLA ŠVANDY ZE SEMČIC, KROFTOVA, ŠTEFÁNIKOVA, ZUBATÉHO, DRTINOVA, Arbesovo náměstí, KOŘENSKÉHO, VOJTĚŠSKÁ, NÁPLAVNÍ, PŠTROSSOVA, Jiráskovo náměstí

→ Map E

D **E** **F** **4**

KAMPA — PETŘÍN HILL

nd son, 1703–55). The imposing church dominates the square without being overpowering: it has an amazingly light touch. Curving galleries, dilated vaults, a big eye-catching cupola: a perfect osmosis between the architectural lines and the opulent rococo décor. Stuccos imitating marble and curving *trompe-l'œil* paintings give the whole an astonishing sense of movement.

Vrtba Garden (D C2)
→ *Karmelitská 18*
April-Oct: Mon-Fri 10am–6pm; Sat-Sun 10am–7pm
n° 25 in the same street, behind a courtyard is one of the most beautiful terraced baroque gardens in Prague (F. M. Kanka, 1720). Loggia decorated with statues from Brokof's workshop. Wonderful view of Malá Strana and the city stretching behind it.

★ **Kampa (D** E2)
Intimate, sheltered from the hubbub of the city, Kampa Island seems enchanted. It is linked to Malá Strana via the little bridges straddling the Devil's Stream, which was once flanked by windmills. On a stroll round its alleys, details grab the eye – a rococo adornment here, a balcony rail there – only adding to the overall charm. Its delightful park offers a stunning view of Charles Bridge and the opposite bank of the Vltava. ★

Maltese Square (D D2)
→ *Maltézské náměstí*
This L-shaped square, untouched by time, bounded by elegant baroque and rococo houses was the dream setting for Miloš Forman's movie *Amadeus*. To the south, the Nostitz Palace, attributed to Caratti.

Velkopřevorské Square (D E2)
A powerful symbol of dissidence lovingly preserved: opposite the imposing baroque portal of the Buquoy Palace, a wall covered with graffiti, including a portrait of John Lennon.

★ **Petřín Hill (D** C3)
→ *Petřínské sady (access via cable car from Újezd)*
On the top, the Belvedere, and a miniature Eiffel Tower built in 1891 for the Universal Exhibition. Nestling in greenery, the baroque St Lawrence's Church (1735- 70) set into the Wall of Hunger built by Charles IV to provide work for the poor. Further south, the Kinský Gardens and the old Orthodox St Michael of Petřín sanctuary (18th century).

WENCESLAS SQUARE

SLAV ISLAND

★ Rotunda of the Holy Cross (**E** A1)
→ *Konviktská/Karoliny*
One of the last gems of Romanesque Prague (12th century). A small chapel with a conical roof, characteristic of the style of the Přemyslids kings (11th-14th centuries). Inside, the remains of Gothic murals (14th century).

★ Národní (**E** A1)
One of the city's liveliest streets, laid in 1871 along the ramparts of the Old Town. At the beginning of the 20th century, the avenue became the favorite strolling ground of the local bourgeoisie. It has preserved its famous cafés, its theaters and its belle époque architectural treasures. Two adjoining buildings by Osvald Polívka reflect the different tendencies of Czech Art Nouveau, At n° 9, the Topič House (1910) is similar to the Germanic *Jugendstil*; at n° 7, the more abstract former Praha Insurance Company Building (1905-07) was influenced by the Viennese Sezession.

★ Church of Our Lady of the Snows (**E** C1)
→ *Jungmannovo náměstí 18*
Tel. 24 22 57 31
Daily 9am–6pm
Commissioned by Charles IV in 1347 to stage his coronation, this would have been Prague's biggest building. However, only the choir was ever finished (in 1379-1397) as religious wars prevented its total completion. Nevertheless, it is still the city's second biggest Gothic church, after the Cathedral. Charming adjacent garden.

★ Wenceslas Square (**E** C1)
Demonstrations against Nazism (1938), the Liberation celebrations (1945), haranguing of Soviet tanks (1968), Jan Palach setting fire to himself (1969) in protest against the repression of the Prague Spring... Twenty years late[r] the square became the stage for the popular ralli[es] of the Velvet Revolution t[hat] hastened the downfall of the Communist regime. The heart of the New Tow[n] (2,460 ft) belongs to the people!

★ Slav Island / Mánes Gallery (**E** A2)
→ *Masarykovo nábřeží 2[5]*
Tel. 24 93 02 23
Tue-Sun 10am–6pm
The Functionalist Mánes Gallery (Otakar Novotný, 1932) links the Masaryk Quay with the southernmost point of Slav Island. It incorporates the Renaissance tower of one

E

TREFENÁ HUSA

FX RADOST

PAVILÓN

CAFÉS

Potrefená Husa (F F3)
→ *Vinohradská and Kolínská 19*
Tel. 6731 0360
Daily 11.30am–1am
The ceiling is red, there is a stadium-like concrete vault and six TV screens hang above the bar. A sporty décor for one of Prague's most delightful cafés, dedicated to the continuance of an old Czech tradition: drinking beer. The service is discreet and friendly and customers can spend hours here drinking one beer without being made to feel ill at ease. Staropramen, Velvet, Kelt on draft. Homemade soups (served in bread), grills, salads.

Kavárna Medúza (F B4)
→ *Belgická 17*
Tel. 2258 534
Mon-Fri 11am–1am;
Sat-Sun noon–1am
Old photos on the walls, comfortable armchairs for long sessions, soft music (classical or cabaret). This café, run by women, has become a neighborhood institution. Salads, sandwiches, a wide

variety of drinks and coffees (Viennese, Irish, Algerian) and a host of cocktails.

BARS, DISCOTHEQUES

U sedmi vlků (F E2)
→ *Vlkova 7*
Tel. 22 71 17 25
Summer: daily 6pm–midnight
Winter: daily 7–11pm
'At the seven wolves' is an inviting café-bar which draws a young, relaxed clientele. Small-scale concerts and DJ sessions in the basement.

Palác Akropolis (F E2)
→ *Kubelíkova 27*
Tel. 296 330 911
www.palacakropolis.cz
A hip alternative cultural center in an old cinema: a café, two bars and a concert hall (see below). Theater shows, indie rock, world music.

Kaaba Café
→ *Tél. 227 12 287*
Mon-Fri 10am–midnight,
Sat-Sun 4pm–1am
A tiny café at the back of the hall provides an intimate space. Velvet on draft, cocktails (such as the very strong *Becherovka* and tonic).

Divaldení bar / Mala scena
→ *Tel. 2272 1031*
Daily 7pm–3am/4am
Every night, from 11pm, DJs rock the joint. A lot of people come here to be seen. Often packed.

FX radost (F B4)
→ *Bělehradská 120*
Tel. 2425 4776
Café-restaurant: daily 11am–3am
Bar: Mon-Fri 9.30–7.30pm; Sat 11am–4pm; Sun 1–5pm
Club: daily 9pm–5am
This is Prague's trendiest techno-house club. The clientele consists of models, young Czech go-getters and Anglo-Saxon dandies, all adept at the art of clubbing, perfectly at ease with the highly sophisticated décor. Difficult for non-members of the tribe to feel at home. Vegetarian restaurant upstairs.

Clan (F B3)
→ *Balbínova 23 (no tel.)*
Daily 7pm–4am
A hymn to the color red. Lights, walls, curtains, sofa, armchairs – all red, from ceiling to floor. Electronic, house and techno music for a young crowd.

Uzi (F A4)
→ *Legerova 44*
Tel. 225 16 036
Daily 8.30pm–5am
The temple of rock. Screenings of films and concerts on a big screen looming over the dance floor.

SHOPPING

U knihomola (F D3)
→ *Mánesova 79*
Tel. 627 7767
Bookstore: Mon-Fri 9am–9pm; Sun 2–9pm
International bookstore, with a good selection of children's books. It is even possible to borrow a book and read it in the basement café. Salads, pizzas and cakes.

Pavilón (F D4)
→ *Vinohradská 50*
Tel. 2209 7111
Mon-Sat 9.30–9pm;
Sun noon–6pm
An old covered market, in a beautiful neo-baroque building with a metal structure, has been converted into a shopping arcade. Major Western brands (Lacoste and Timberland), but also an Italian café and a big grocery store in the basement.

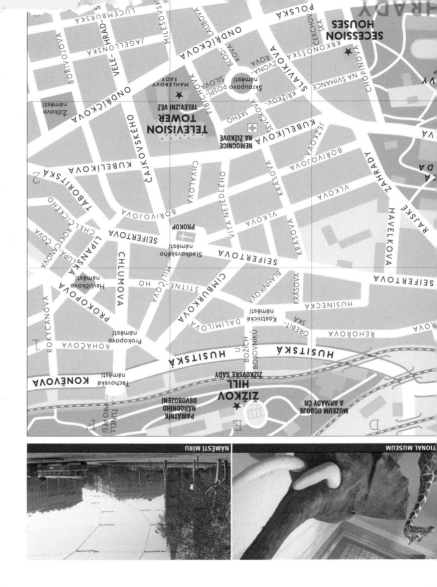

URCH OF THE SACRED HEART

TELEVISION TOWER

ŽIŽKOV HILL

Náměstí Míru (**F** B4)
e layout of the Peace
quare reflects a
erarchical approach to
y planning, organized
ound a space containing
e Vinohrady Theater
905–07), a neo-baroque
ilding with Jugendstil
coration; and the neo-
thic Church of Saint
dmila (1888–93). The
ter served as a meeting
ace during the Velvet
volution, and its two
tagonal 194-ft towers can
seen for miles around.
Secession houses
D3)
Mánesova/Chopinova/
Švihance/Krkoniška

Take an architectural stroll
between Mánesova and the
eastern side of Riegrovy
Park to discover the
Secession style.
Ornamentation rules, and
it is integrated into the
buildings' very structures.
At nº 4 on Chopinova, the
Jan Kotěra House (1908–
09): imposing bow-window
and daring redbrick
decoration. At nº 6, the
Bohumil Waigant House
(1909–10): angular
architecture marking the
transition to the geometri-
cal phase of the Secession
style. At nº 3 on Na
Švihance, the L. Čapek
House (1907–08):

remarkable bow window.
Beautiful views of the city
from Riegrovy Park.
★ **Church of the Sacred
Heart** (**F** E3)
→ Ke Karlovu 20
Tel. 24 92 33 63
Tue–Sun 10am–5pm
Vitrified brick façade, big
bell tower, huge glass clock,
large nave designed as a
single form. This is a dis-
tinctive building (1927–33)
and the major work in
Prague by the Slovenian
architect Josip Plečník.
★ **Television Tower** (**F** E2)
→ Malherovy sady 1
Tel. 627 34 97
Daily 10am–11pm
Futuristic tower (1985–

1992) looking down
on the city from 708 ft.
Remarkable panorama of
Žižkov and Vinohrady from
its viewing platform.
★ **Žižkov Hill** (**F** E1)
In July 1420 the Hussites,
led by Jan Žižka, defeated
the forces of Emperor
Sigismund on Vítkov Hill.
In 1877, the hill was
renamed Žižkov and in
1950 Bohumil Kafka
unveiled a monumental
equestrian statue of the
Czech patriot. Behind him,
the Constructivist National
Monument (1925–32)
stands as a symbol of the
Czech people's struggles
for independence.

BUS STATIONS

Praha–Florenc
→ M° Florenc
International lines
(Capital Express,
Tourbus, BEI) and
internal journeys.
Information
→ Tel. 24 21 10 60
Tickets, bookings
Best prices in agencies
(Čedok).
Želivského
Eurolines (London)
→ Tel. 01582 404 511
Other stations
Želivského (subway line
A), Holešovice (subway
line B), Smíchov (subway
line B), Palmovka
(subway line C).

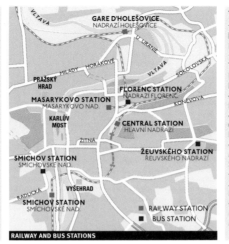

RAILWAY AND BUS STATIONS

TRAIN STATIONS

Hlavní Nádraží
Prague's main station.
15 min on foot from Old
Town Square. Subway
line C.
Information
→ Tel. 2422 3887
Reservations
→ Tél. 2421 7040
Other stations
Nádraží Holešovice
→ rains from northern
Europe Subway line C
Smíchov
→ International trains
Subway line B
Masarykovo
→ Regional lines
(Bohemia, Brno and
Bratislava)

secret police prison under
the Communist regime, is
now run by nuns and has
regained its serenity.
1,200 Kč without bathroom.
Pension Vyšehrad (E C6)
→ Krokova 6
Tel. 42 48 13
www.praguehotels.cz
Calm and hospitality in
a small family hotel two
streets from Vyšehrad
subway station. Ring the
bell for 'Kovarikova'.
1,650 Kč.
Pension Avalon (A D2)
→ Havelská 15
Tel. 06 02 14 41 89
In a 15th-century house
near Saint Havel's market.
Small, simple but clean
rooms, all with bathroom.
Young clientele (possibility
of sharing rooms for 4/5
people). 1,200-1,700 Kč.
Pension City (F B4)
→ Belgická 10
Tel. 2252 1606
Access Namesti Miru subway
Quiet, bright and well-

equipped rooms, decorated
in somewhat passé 1960s
style. 30% discount for stay
of three days (from Sunday
to Tuesday). 1,550 Kč.
Pension U Lilie (A C2)
→ Liliová 15
Tel. 2222 0432
An anonymous entrance
and charming sunny
courtyard just a few
minutes from Charles
Bridge. Seventeen simple
but bright rooms, some
overlooking the courtyard.
Restaurant 1,500-2,500 Kč.
Pension Větrník
→ U Větrníku 40
Tel. 20 51 33 90
Tram n° 18
A mere half hour suffices to
escape from the center and
breathe some country air.
Six large guest rooms (big
beds, down duvets) in an
18th-century mill owned by
Miloš Opatmý. Medieval
cellar (or courtyard in
summer) for genuine
Czech meals by a fireplace.

Booking essential.
2,000 Kč.

2,000–3,000 Kč

U Medvídků (A C3)
→ Na Perštýne 7
Tel. 2421 1916
One of the biggest and
oldest bars in Prague
(4 large rooms) also has
22 bedrooms in a pseudo-
Gothic style.
2,000–3,000 Kč.
Hotel Evropa (E C1)
→ Vaclavské námestí 25
Tel. 2422 8117
Art Nouveau at its most
luxurious and decadent.
The Evropa may have lost
its sheen but its charm
persists (revolving door,
wooden elevator).
Magnificent coffee room
with wood trim (live music
at nights). Fittings vary
from room to room.
2,600–3,900 Kč.
Hotel Lunik (F B4)
→ Londýnská 50

Tel. 2425 3974
The 'socialist realism' of the
Lunik's facade stands out
in a pretty English-style
street (rows of identical
little houses with front
gardens). The interior,
however, is cozy, and the
welcome is friendly: 35
rooms, bar, garden, sauna,
solarium and restaurant-
gallery displaying works by
Czech and Russian artists.
2,200–2,500 Kč.
Hotel U Krále Jiřího (A C2)
→ Liliová 10
Tel. 2222 0925
Legend has it that a Knight
Templar still wanders the
premises with his head
under his arm. The 14th-
century 'King George'
provides the perfect
medieval setting to wait
for his appearance.
Twelve rooms with beautiful
dark wooden furnishings.
Pub in the vaulted
basement. 2,700-3,350 Kč.
Hotel 16 (E C4)

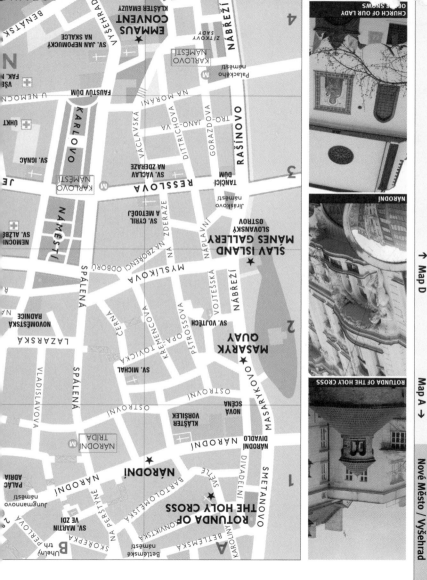

CHURCH OF OUR LADY OF THE SNOWS

NÁRODNÍ

ROTUNDA OF THE HOLY CROSS

EMMAUS CONVENT

KLÁŠTER EMAUZY

SV. JAN NEPOMUCKÝ NA SKALCE

VYŠEHRAD

BENÁTSKÁ

NÁBŘEŽÍ

ZÍTKOVY SADY

KARLOVO NÁMĚSTÍ M

Palackého náměstí

FAUSTŮV DŮM

KARLOVO

NA MORÁNI

U NEMOCN

VŠE FAK. N

ÚHKT

SV. IGNÁC

VÁCLAVSKÁ

JANO-VA

VACLAVSKÁ

DITTRICHOVA

TRO-JANO-VA

GORAZDOVA

RAŠÍNOVO

JE

NÁMĚSTÍ

KARLOVO NÁMĚSTÍ M

RESSLOVA

SV. VÁCLAV NA ZDERAZE

Tančící DŮM

Jiráskovo náměstí

NEMOCNI SV. ALŽB

SPÁLENÁ

SV. CYRIL A METODĚJ

NA ZDERAZE

NAPLAVNÍ

SLOVANSKÝ OSTROV

SLAV ISLAND

MÁNES GALLERY

MYSLÍKOVA

VOJTĚŠSKÁ

NÁBŘEŽÍ

NOVOMĚSTSKÁ RADNICE

LAZARSKÁ

VLADISLAVOVA

SPÁLENÁ

ČERNÁ

KREMENCOVA

OPATOVICKÁ

PŠTROSSOVA

SV. VOJTĚCH

MASARYK QUAY

SV. MICHAL

OSTROVNÍ

OSTROVNÍ

NOVÁ SCÉNA

KLÁŠTER VORŠILEK

MASARYKOVO

NÁRODNÍ TŘÍDA M

NÁRODNÍ

NÁRODNÍ DIVADLO

DIVADELNÍ

SMETANOVO

PALÁC ADRIA

Jungmannovo náměstí

NÁRODNÍ

BARTOLOMĚJSKÁ

ROTUNDA OF THE HOLY CROSS

SV. MARTIN VE ZDI

NA PERŠTÝNĚ

KONVIKTSKÁ

BETLÉMSKÁ

KAROLINY SVĚTLÉ

Uhelný trh PERLOVÁ

ŠKORÉPKA

Betlémské náměstí

B

A

N

Wide avenues, elegant hundred-year-old galleries, monumental squares: the 'New Town', born of a big 14th-century planning project, revolves around the enormous Wenceslas Square, once the focus of Czech opposition to the Soviet occupation. Na příkopě and Národní teem with restaurants, cafés and stores. To the south of Nové Město lies the legendary cradle of the princes of Bohemia, the 'other' castle, perched on Vyšehrad Hill and overlooking the Vltava. You can reach it by walking up Vratislava St and as with many other places in Prague the visit is a magical trip back in time, far from the bustle of the center. At the foot of the hill are Josef Chochol's Cubist buildings.

CAFÉ SLAVIA CAFÉ PATIO

RESTAURANTS

Dynamo (**E** A2)
→ *Pštrossova 220/29*
Tel. 2493 2020
Daily 10am–midnight
Designer furniture and minimal decoration (manga posters) in a setting to match its young, hip clientele. Salads and big plates of pasta. Dishes 100 Kč. Or simply sit at the bar, trying one of the 70 whiskies on offer (100–2,000 Kč).

Le Bistrot de Marlène (**E** A5)
→ *Plavecká 4*
Tel. 2492 1853
Mon-Fri noon–2.30pm, 7–10.30pm;
Sat 2.30 7pm–10.30pm
Since 1995 Marlène Salomon has regaled her customers (both locals and tourists) with simple but hearty French cooking. The key to her success: the irreproachable freshness of the ingredients. The menu varies according to the season. Provençal décor, bathed with natural light. Dish of the day 300 Kč.

La Perle de Prague (**E** A3)
→ *Rašínovo nábřeží 80*
Tel. 219 84 160

Tue-Sat noon–2pm, 7–10.30pm; Mon 7–10.30pm
Bar: 9am–2am
On the 7th floor of the 'dancing house', the highly controversial building by the Canadian architect Frank Gehry. The cuisine is refined and excellent, but perhaps not as spectacular as the views of the Vltava, the Castle and Petřín Hill. Terrace in summer. À la carte 900–2,000 Kč (lunch menu 490 Kč).

CZECH PUB

U pinkasů (**E** B1)
→ *Jungmannovo náměstí 15/16. Tel. 242 22 965*
Daily 9am–11pm
One of the few taverns in the city center that has retained its authenticity. Smoky atmosphere, clinking tankards, old regulars leaning on the bar. Pilsner Urquell has been sold here on draft since 1843. Price 30 Kč.

CAFÉS, INTERNET CAFÉ, TEAROOM

Café Slavia (**E** A1)
→ *Smetanovo 2*
Tel. 24 22 09 57
Mon-Fri 8am–midnight;
Sat-Sun 9am–midnight
Smetana, Dvořák, Havel:

AIRPORT

Ruzyně airport
13 miles west of Prague.
Information
→ *Tel. 2011 1111*
Links to city center
Bus
→ *Line n° 119*
Every 10 mins to Dejvicka subway (45 mins trip)
Price 8–12 Kč (bus ticket)
ČA minibus
→ *Every day to Dejvicka subway or center.*
Price 30 Kč (30 mins trip)
Cedaz
→ *5.30am–9.30pm*
Every day. Price 92 Kč
Taxi Fix Car
→ *500 Kč (20 mins trip)*
Possibility of sharing a taxi.

N
↑
13 miles
PRAGUE
RUZYNĚ   PRAGUE

AIRPORT

TAXIS

A fare scale (displayed on the front doors) has been introduced but Prague's taxis are still unreliable.
→ *Starting fare 30 Kč then 22 Kč/km (waiting 4 Kč/min)*
Companies
The following companies speak English.
AAA Taxi
→ *Tel. 1080*
ProfiTaxi
→ *Tel. 1035*

CARS

Driving is not advisable in the center (pedestrian areas, one-way streets).
Alcohol levels
Zero tolerance of drinking and driving.
Speed
50 km/hr in town,
90 km/hr in rural areas,
130 km/hr on freeway.
Parking
Three paying zones from Mon–Sat, 8am–6pm.
Orange zone
→ *Price 10 Kč/15 mins, 40 Kč/1hr (limit 2 hrs)*
Green zone
→ *Price 30 Kč/hr, 120 Kč/6 hrs (limit 6 hrs)*
Blue zone
→ *Residents and businesses*
Parking lots
City center
→ *Price 30 Kč/hr, approx. 340 Kč/day*
Outskirts (P+R)
→ *Supervised parking Price 10 Kč/day.*
Infringements
Clamp: phone the n° indicated on the ticket; the authorities remove it for a minimum of 500 Kč.

Except where otherwise indicated, the prices given are for a double room with bathroom, breakfast included. As most hotels have no more than a dozen rooms, it is essential to book several weeks in advance for April to October, Christmas, Easter and weekends.

YOUTH HOSTELS

Hostel Sokol (D D3)
→ *Újezd 40-450*
Tel. 5700 7397. June–Sep
This big building, opposite Petřín Park and close to Malá Strana, serves as a sport school in winter and a youth hostel in summer. Big terrace and bright, spacious dormitories with 12 beds.
190 Kč/ person.
Klub Habitat (E B2)
→ *Na Zbořenci 10*
Tel. 290 315
The profits from this

hostel, in a beautiful 19th-century bourgeois building, finance charity projects for children. Clean, bright dormitories (3–6 beds). 350–500 Kč per person.
Traveller's hostel-Pension Dlouhá (B C4)
→ *Dlouhá 33*
Tel. 2482 6662
Central hostel open all year round, popular with American tourists. Close to the *Roxy*, a Prague rock institution.
1,160 Kč double room; 320–550 Kč/person in dormitory.
Kolej AMU (B D3)
→ *Hradební, 7*
Tel. 2251 1777
Musical atmosphere in a building in the old ghetto that also houses the Music Academy.
A few beds outside summer season.
Dormitory 400 Kč/person; double room 700 Kč.

Pension Košická
→ *Košická 12*
Tel. 7174 2483
Access tram n°. 22
In this huge house near Havlíckovy Park, rooms with 2 to 6 beds.
300–800 Kč/person in dormitory.
Domov Mládeže Penzion Jana (F F4)
→ *Dykova 20*
Tel. 2251 1777
In a haven of green space in Vinohrady, a big building with large but cozy rooms.
From 250 Kč/person, dorms with 6 beds.

1,000–2,000 Kč

Unitas Pension (A C3)
→ *Bartolomějská 9*
Tel. 2421 1020
For anybody wishing to spend a night in the cell where Vaclav Havel once slept (room P6). The former convent, later a

Transport and hotels in Prague

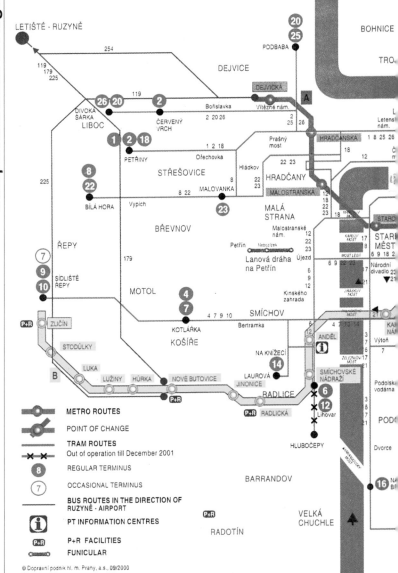

© Dopravní podnik hl. m. Prahy, a.s., 09/2000

LRYBA

KORUNA PALÁC

LUCERNA PASÁŽ

ever since 1863 writers, musicians and dissident intellectuals have packed the benches of this legendary café. The closure of this former bastion of dissent in 1992 aroused fierce protests from President Havel, among others. The Slavia finally reopened in 1998 and its 'absinthe-green' Art Deco interior still has a magnetic attraction – for tourists, businessmen and old Czech ladies. Have tea with pastries and revel in the wonderful atmosphere. Big bay windows opening out on to the river. Enter via Národní. Coffee, pastries 25–30 Kč.

Café Patio (E B1)
→ *Národní 22*
Tel. 249 18 072 (café)
Daily 10am–9pm
Tel. 249 21 060 (store)
Daily 10am–7pm
Redbrick walls, dark wooden furniture, wrought-iron lamps. The bric-à-brac décor provides a relaxed setting for meeting a friend over a drink or snack. Good choice of cafés and pastries. Store in the basement: wrought-iron pieces, chandeliers.

Café Louvre (E B1)
→ *Národní 20*

Tel. 297 223 / 2493 0949
Daily 8am–11pm
One of Prague's most elegant cafés, where Franz Kafka and Max Brod used to meet. On the first floor, three bright, spacious rooms. Coffee, tea, pastries, meals, all served with style by waiters in white aprons.

**Electra Internet Café
(E** A3)
→ *Rašínovo nábřeží 62*
Tel. 297 038
www.electra.cz
Mon-Fri 9am–1am;
Sat-Sun 11am–midnight
Large café with 15 computers (access at 1 Kč/min). To drink: 13 types of coffees, beers.

Dobrá čajovna (E C1)
→ *Václavské náměstí 14*
Tel. 311 64 79
Mon-Sat 10am–9.30pm;
Sun 3pm–9.30pm
Enjoy a well-deserved break from the bustle of Wenceslas Square. A variety of teas (China, Taiwan, Japan, Africa).

BARS, JAZZ CLUBS, CONCERT VENUES

Velryba (E A2)
→ *Opatovická 24*
Tel. 249 12 391
Daily 11am–2am (midnight Sun)
'The whale', the city's

first café-gallery, opened in 1989. At lunchtime, students and young artists come to read a newspaper over a coffee or a plate of pasta. At night, alcohol and tobacco take over. The second room provides more intimacy. Gallery in the basement. Gambrinus (bottle) and strong liquor.
Dishes 100 Kč.

**Lucerna Music Bar
(E** C1)
→ *Vodičkova 36*
Tel. 24 21 71 08
Coffeeshop: daily 11am–5pm / Bar daily 8pm–3am
Concerts: 9pm
In a basement, on two levels, a bar, a concert hall, with uninhibited Czech regulars who come to discover the best local or international groups (1960s rock, disco, blues, reggae, jazz). Admission 60–300 Kč. The hall is borrowed every Oct by the Prague Jazz Festival.

Agharta (E C2)
→ *Krakovská 5*
Tel. 24 21 29 14
Daily 9am–midnight
This club, founded in 1991, is for true jazz lovers. Foreign and Czech musicians (e.g. Jiří Stívin , flute, Karel Růžička sax) play here. Warm, intimate

setting. Jazz CDs on sale at the door.

Rock Café (E B1)
→*Národní 20*
Tel. 24 91 44 16
Mon-Fri 8pm–3am
Concerts: daily 9pm
One of the pioneers of underground rock, it has gone on to greater things. Concert hall, cinema, CD store, Internet corner. Pretty deserted during the day.

SHOPPING

Koruna Palác (E C1)
→ *Václavské náměstí (corner Na příkope)*
Tel. 24 21 95 26
Mon-Sat 9am–8pm;
Sun 10am–6pm
Shopping center in a beautiful *Jugendstil* building. In the basement, the biggest record store in town.

Lucerna pasáž (E C1)
Magnificent shopping passageway (1912–16), built by Václav Havel's grandfather.

Galery Mody
→ *Štěpánská 61*
Tel. 2421 1514
On the first floor of the passage, clothes by Czech designers like Helena Fejková (linen clothes). Small café in the entrance.

← Map D   ↑ Map F

MASARYK QUAY

DVOŘÁK MUSEUM

EMMAUS CONVENT

↓ Map A

NOVÉ MĚSTO (PRAHA 2)

SV. APOLINÁŘ · APOLINÁŘSKÁ · VINIČNÁ · KE KARLI

KOUBKOVA · Fügnerovo náměstí · KE KARLOVU

TYRŠOVA · KATEŘINSKÁ

SOKOLSKÁ · BĚLE-HRADSKÁ · RUMUNSKÁ · LEGEROVA

MUZEUM ANTONÍNA DVOŘÁKA
DVOŘÁK MUSEUM
★ SV. KATEŘINA · NA BOJIŠTI

LUBLAŇSKÁ · LONDÝNSKÁ · I.P. PAVLOVA Ⓜ náměstí I.P. Pavlova

LIPOVÁ

JUGOSLÁVSKÁ · BĚLEHRADSKÁ · VOCELOVA · MIKOVCOVA · LEGEROVA

JEČNÁ · KE KARLOVU

ANGLICKÁ · MEZIBRANSKÁ

ROTUNDA SV. LONGINA · V TŮNÍCH · HÁLKOVA · SV. ŠTĚPÁN · ŠTĚPÁNSKÁ · NA RYBNÍČKU

ŽITNÁ

ŠKRÉTOVA · RUBEŠOVA · ŘÍMSKÁ

LEGEROVA

NÁRODNÍ MUZEUM

VINOHRADSKÁ

KRAKOVSKÁ · VE SMEČKÁCH · ŠTĚPÁNSKÁ · V JÁMĚ · ŠKOLSKÁ · VODIČKOVA

STÁTNÍ OPERA · WASHINGTONOVA · Ⓜ MUZEUM náměstí Václavské

WILSONOVA · OPLETALOVA

LUCERNA

WENCESLAS SQUARE VÁCLAVSKÉ NÁMĚSTÍ

CHURCH OF OUR LADY OF THE SNOWS · MARIA SNĚŽNA · náměstí Václavské

OPLETALOVA · POLITICKÝCH VĚZŇŮ · OLIVOVA · JINDŘIŠSKÁ · RŮŽOVA

POŠTA · Ⓜ MŮSTEK

CUBIST HOUSES

VYŠEHRAD

water deposits that once
pplied the city's public
untains. Contemporary art
hibition. Pleasant strolls
Slav Island Park.

Masaryk Quay (**E** A2)
autiful collection of neo-
naissance, neo-baroque
d Art Nouveau buildings.
not miss n° 32, with
lovely entrance on the
rner of the Goethe
stitute (Jiri Stibral 1904–
); remarkable stuccos by
lda Klouček at n° 26.
Dvořák Museum (**E** C3)
Ke Karlovu, 20
24 92 33 63
e-Sun 10am–5pm
e Amerika Villa, an
egant baroque house by

Kilián Ignác Dientzenhofer
(1720), has contained the
Dvořák Museum since 1932.
Original scores, letters,
former possessions of the
famous composer, born to
the north of Prague in
Nelahozeves.

★ **Emmaus Convent/
St John-Nepomuk-on-the-
Rock** (**E** B4)
→ Vyšehradská 49
Tel. 24 91 53 71
Severely tested by the
Hussite wars (1420), the
sanctuaries now only show
a few traces of their Gothic
murals. The fragments of
frescoes (14th century) kept
in the cloister of Emmaus
Convent are some of the

most beautiful in Bohemia.
Just opposite, perched on a
rock, a tiny church devoted
to St John Nepomuk, one
of the treasures of baroque
art (K. I. Dientzenhofer,
1730–49).

★ **Cubist houses** (**E** A5)
→ Neklanova 30/Libušina 3/
Rašínovo nábřeží 6-8-10
Prague is the only city in the
world to have developed
this type of architecture.
Several examples on the
foot of Vyšehrad Hill by
Josef Chochol (1880–1956).
Masterpiece: the Kovařovič
villa (Libušina 3), built on
a triangular site in 1913.
Spectacular corner pillar
on the apartment building

(Neklanova 30) situated at
the junction of two streets.
★ **Vyšehrad** (**E** B6)
Legend has it that Princess
Libuše built Prague Castle
on Vyšehrad Hill in 717 after
having a vision. She chose
a husband by the name of
Přemysl, and they started
the Přemyslid dynasty
(which lasted until 1306).
Vyšehrad became the
stronghold of the first kings
of Bohemia, although it was
later replaced by Hradčany.
Stunning views from the
park and the ramparts of
the fortress. Some of the
nation's greatest artists
(Smetana, Dvořák, Mucha)
rest in the cemetery (1870).

SECESSION HOUSE, MÁNESOVA

SECESSION HOUSES, VINHORADSKÁ

★ Mucha Museum (F A2)
→ Panská 7. Tel. 628 41 62
Daily 10am–6pm (guided tours on request)
www.mucha.cz
The life and work of the most widely known Czech artist. In 1895, Alfons Mucha (1860–1939) became famous through a poster designed for a Sarah Bernhardt's theater play and set off for Paris, where he launched the Art Nouveau style: floral and vegetal motifs, female figures with endlessly flowing hair. Back in Prague in 1910, he helped decorate the Town Hall and then designed the stained-glass windows for St Vitus' Cathedral. His last work was the Slav Epic, a cycle of 20 enormous paintings. The 5,400 s ft of floor space embrace the various facets of Mucha's talent (posters, decorative panels, pastels, paintings, drawings, sketches). Store (sale of reproductions).

★ Central Station (F B2)
→ Hlavní nádraží/Wilsonová 8. Tel. 24 22 38 87
The city's largest building in the Secession style (1901–09), after the Town Hall. Josef Fanta (1856–1954) let his imagination run wild, with colors and ornamental details tumbling over each other, especially in the semi-circular dome.

★ State Opera (F B3)
→ Wilsonová 84
Tel. 24 22 76 93
Mon-Fri 10am–5.30pm; Sat-Sun 10am–noon, 1–5.30pm
Spurred on by the monumental National Theater whose foundation stone was laid in 1868, Prague's German community commissioned two Austrian architects to build a 'German theater'. In 1888 this exact, though smaller, copy of the Vienna Opera House (and of Prague's biggest theaters) opened, staging operas by Strauss and symphonies by Mahler. Today's repertoire includes foreign operas.

★ National Museum (F A3)
→ Václavské náměstí 68
Tel. 24 49 71 11
Daily 9am–5pm
Closed 1st Mon of month
Founded in 1918 in a wave of Czech patriotism, like the National Theater, the Museum embodies the nationalist revival. It contains precious medieval documents (library), stones and meteorites (ground floor), collections of Czech minerals, zoology and paleontology (1st floor).

F

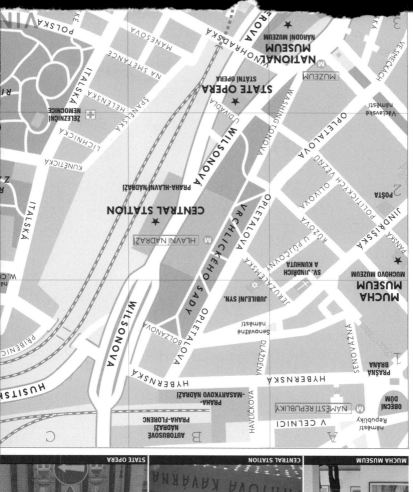

STATE OPERA

CENTRAL STATION

MUCHA MUSEUM

Big parks, tree-lined avenues, sophisticated Secession and Art Nouveau buildings: the former royal vineyards of Vinohrady, planted by Charles IV in the 14th century, were built up at the end of the 19th century to provide residences for the Czech bourgeoisie. Vinohrady is now mutating again, and becoming less residential in the process, as some of the city's most select bars and nightclubs have opened here to attract the local trendsetters. Further to the east lies Žižkov (named after the Hussite chief Jan Žižka). The rundown concrete houses of this former working-class stronghold now serve as venues for a burgeoning alternative scene.

RESTAURACE TELEVIZNÍ VĚŽ

KAVÁRNA MEDÚZA

RESTAURANTS

Český svět (F A3)
→ *Žitná 42*
Tel. 24 94 17 57
Daily noon–midnight
A small restaurant, reminiscent of a canteen. Customers sit in lines to eat simple and filling dishes like *rizote komančero* (rice, chicken, beans and cheese). The place is difficult to find (entrance on the left in the building's passageway).
Around 100 Kč.

Ambiente (F D3)
→ *Mánesova 59*
Tel. 6275 913 922
Mon-Fri 11am–midnight; Sat-Sun 1pm–midnight
Barbecue cooking and 14 types of fresh pasta (fettuccine, tortellini, gnocchi, etc.). Often full, so it is worth booking. Grills 200 Kč, pasta 100 Kč.

Restaurace televizní věž (F E2)
→ *Mahlerovy sady 1*
Tel. 6700 5766
Daily 11am–11pm
Eat at the top of the television tower for a breathtaking view of the Vinohrady and Žižkov neighborhoods. International cuisine.
Dishes 100–200 Kč.

Ponte (F B4)
→ *Anglická 15*
Tel. 24 22 16 65
Daily 11.30am–11pm
Classic but sophisticated Czech specialties like *svíčková na smetaně* (roast beef with cream and blueberries). In winter, try to find a spot near the fireplace. Wide range of cocktails and wines.
Dishes 400–500 Kč.

CZECH PUB

U Vystřeleného oka (F E1)
→ *U Božích Bojovníků 3*
Tél. 627 87 14
Mon-Sat 3.30pm–1am
The décor of this charming rustic tavern, at the end of a cul-de-sac in the Žižkov neighborhood, has been given a satirical edge, humorously evoking the Hussite era, by the young artist Martin Velisek. Mixed clientele, characteristic of the area. Radegast and Velkopopovický on draft, to accompany *utopenec* (Czech sausage and onion marinated in vinegar, 80 Kč). Strong liquor, wines.)

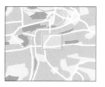

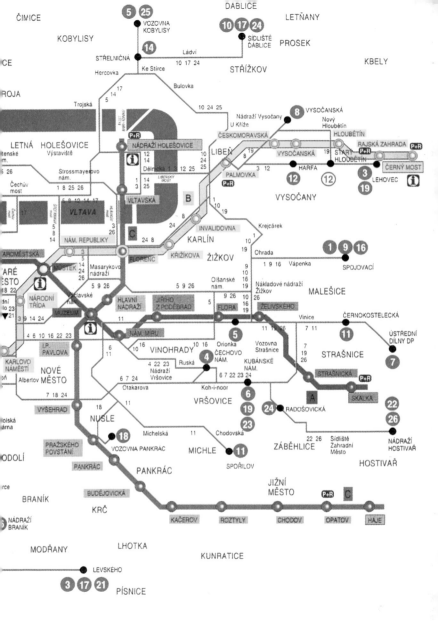